HOAGY CARMICHAEL
EASY PIANO SONGBOOK

W9-ATI-956

FOREWORD

As a young boy, I often heard my father playing his "standards"; the songs of his that everyone else in the English-speaking world seemed to enjoy. I too had my favorites, and those mostly had catchy lyrics, or rhythms that caught my fancy. Dad would often play the songs of his that were rolling around in his head, or a request or two, when people came to the house for an evening. My list of favorites seldom got a nod.

That changed when dad began working on a growing list of children's songs in the early 1950s. He collected poems and lyrics with themes that he felt children would enjoy, and began writing the music for those words when time would allow. He played them all for me and my brother Randy, and we got an early window into an extraordinary collection of songs for children. He later recorded an album of many of the songs, and a songbook was published, but for forty years after that these wonderful little songs languished.

It pleases me very much that the people at Hal Leonard have agreed to re-publish these songs for children. They deserve an airing, and I know that my father would be very pleased that they are once again finding their way to people's piano stands. And, like those evenings at our house fifty years ago, there are some of dad's evergreen songs included in this folio to please the tastes of every generation.

Hoagy Bix Carmichael
3/20/01

Cover photo courtesy of Archives of Traditional Music
at Indiana University

ISBN 0-634-01663-6

HAL•LEONARD®
CORPORATION
7777 W. BLUEMOUND RD. P.O. BOX 13819 MILWAUKEE, WI 53213

Visit Hal Leonard Online at
www.halleonard.com

BUSTIN' OUT OF DOORS

Words and Music by
HOAGY CARMICHAEL

I Get Along Without You Very Well

Inspired by a poem written by
J. B. THOMPSON

Arranged, transcribed and orchestrated by Tom Fay

Words and Music by
HOAGY CARMICHAEL

2

shel - tered in your arms, of course I do. But I get a - long with - out you ver - y well. I've for - got - ten you just like I should, of course I have; ex - cept to hear your name or some - one's laugh that is the same. But I've for - got - ten

4

out you ver-y well, of course I do; ex-cept per-

haps in spring, but I should nev-er think of spring for that would sure-ly

break my heart in two.

Soon there'll be a cir-cus, and if the neigh-bors work us, We can make e-nough to buy some

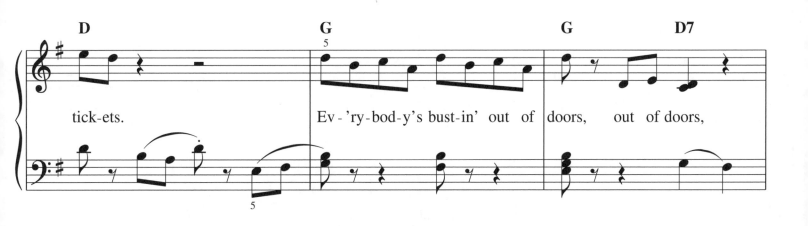

tick-ets. Ev-'ry-bod-y's bust-in' out of doors, out of doors,

Not a soul I know stays put; Now's the time to wear your shorts and

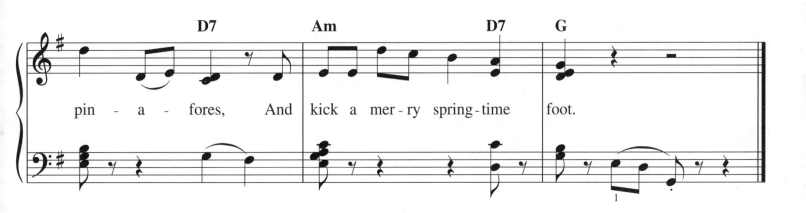

pin - a - fores, And kick a mer - ry spring - time foot.

CLOUDS

Music by HOAGY CARMICHAEL
Words by CHRISTINA GEORGINA ROSSETTI

COMRADES

Music by HOAGY CARMICHAEL
Words by AGNES LOUISE DEAN

COOKING

Words and Music by
HOAGY CARMICHAEL

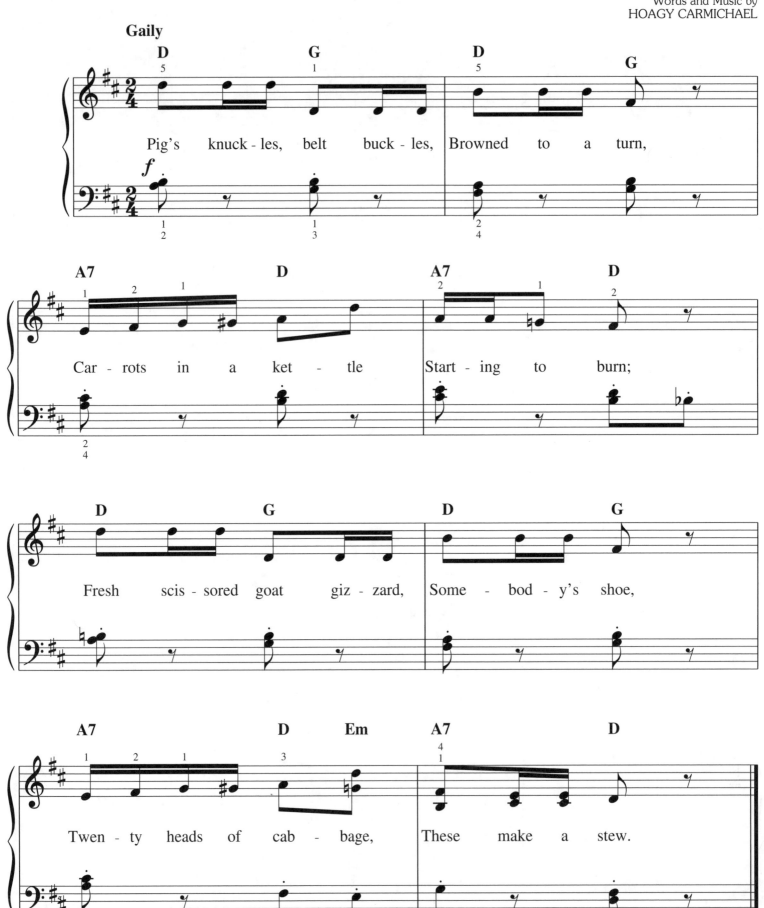

GEORGIA ON MY MIND

Words by STUART GORRELL
Music by HOAGY CARMICHAEL

Moderately slow

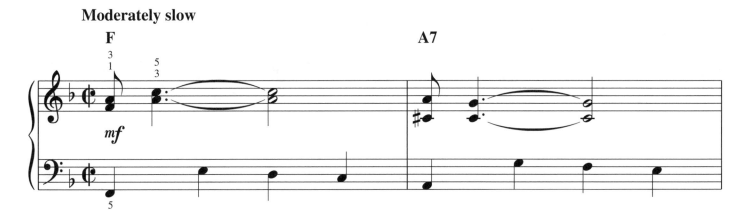

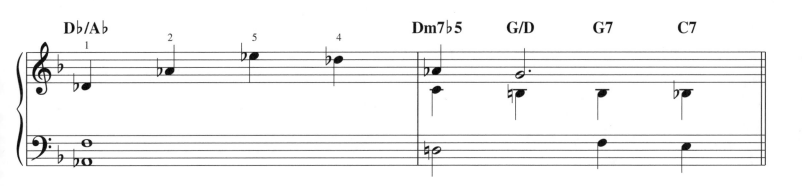

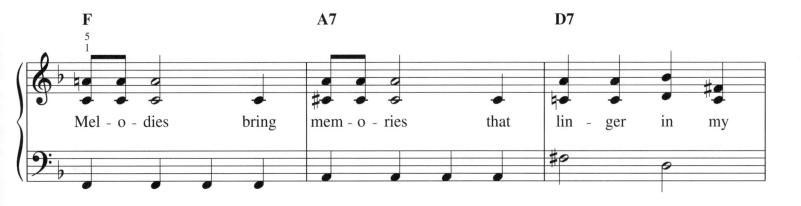

Mel - o - dies bring mem - o - ries that lin - ger in my

heart. _____ Make me think of Geor - gia, why

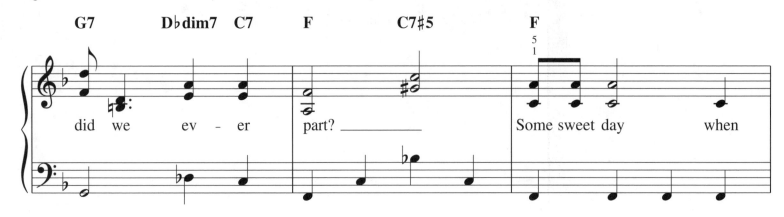

did we ev - er part? _____ Some sweet day when

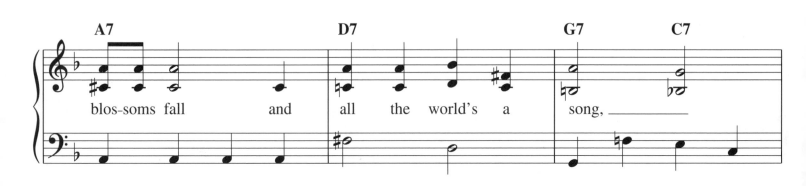

blos-soms fall and all the world's a song, _____

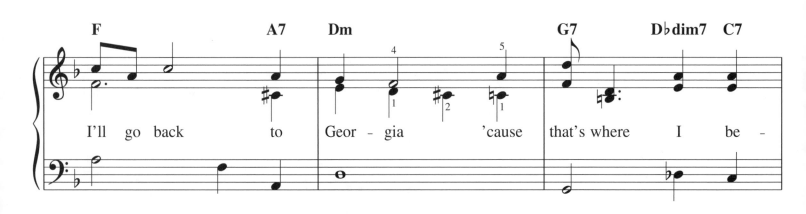

I'll go back to Geor - gia 'cause that's where I be -

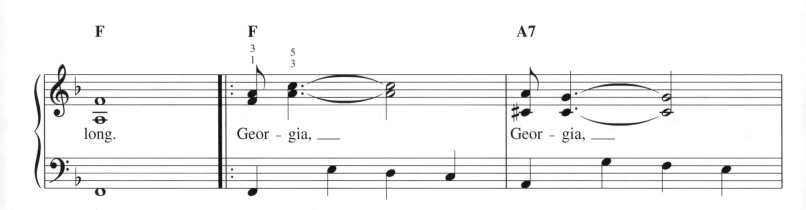

long. Geor - gia, ___ Geor - gia, ___

9

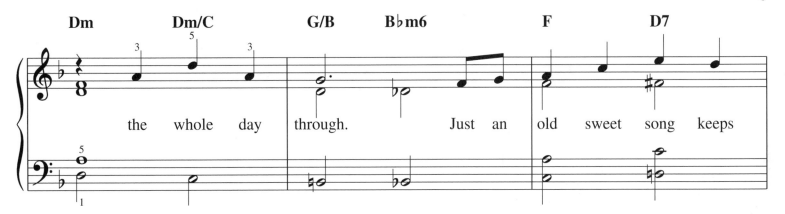

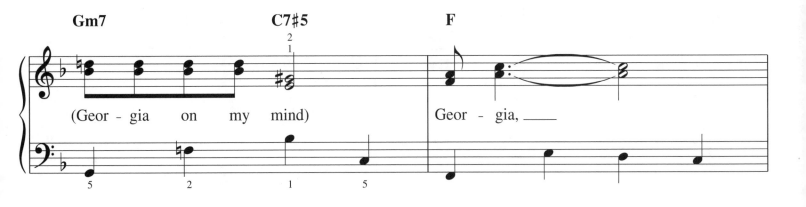

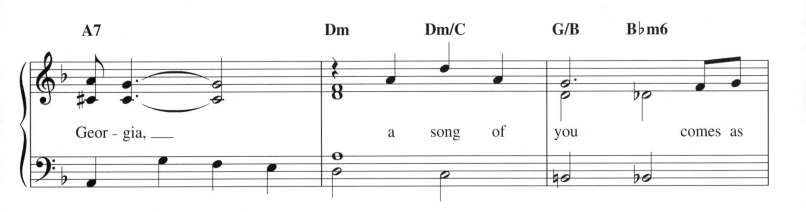

10

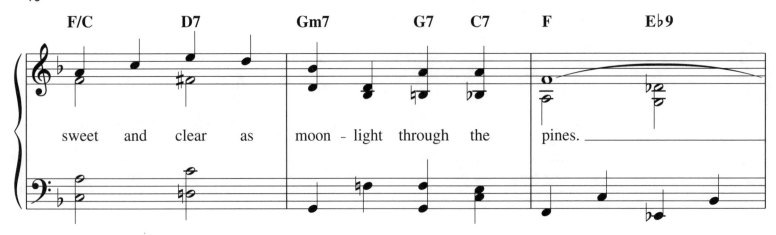

sweet and clear as moon - light through the pines. _____

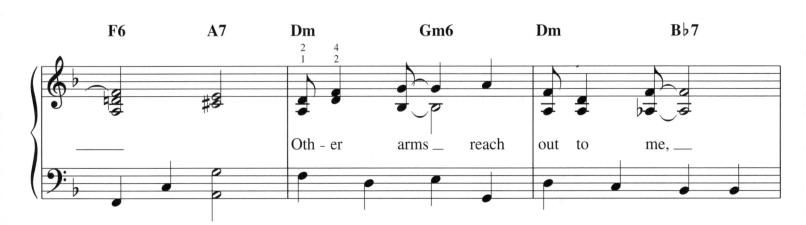

_____ Oth - er arms ___ reach out to me, ___

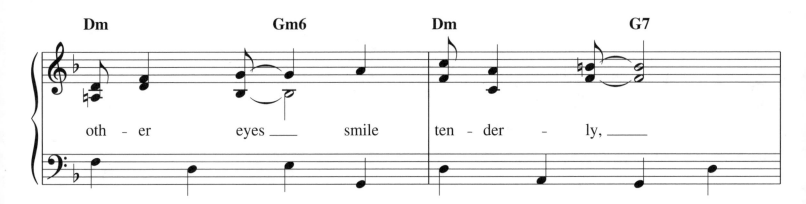

oth - er eyes ___ smile ten - der - ly, ___

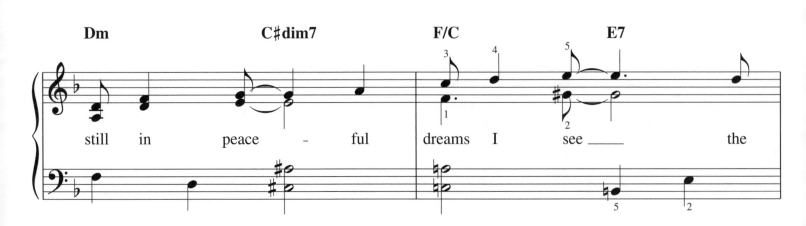

still in peace - ful dreams I see ___ the

11

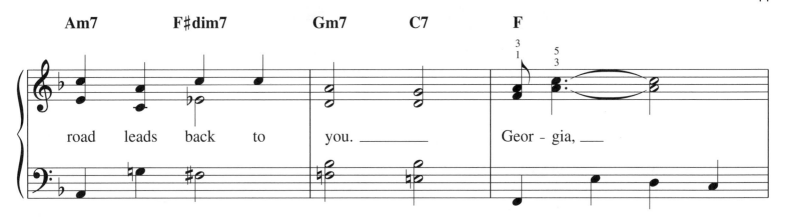

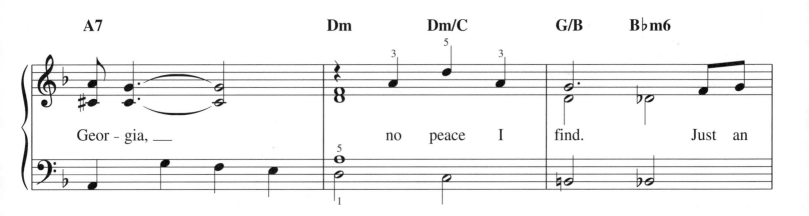

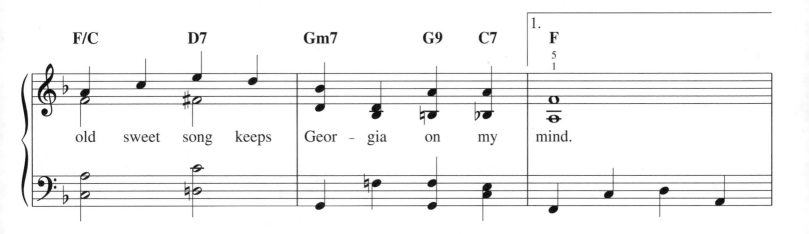

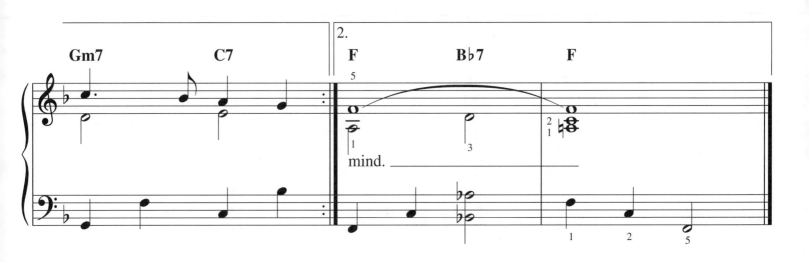

HEART AND SOUL
from the Paramount Short Subject A SONG IS BORN

Words by FRANK LOESSER
Music by HOAGY CARMICHAEL

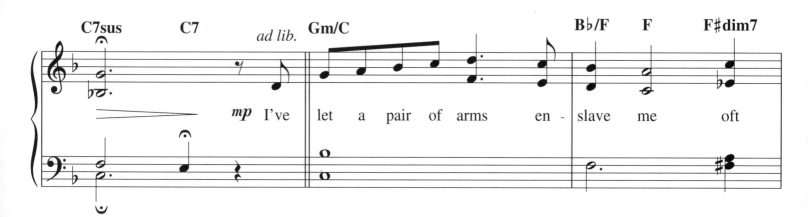

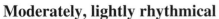

Moderately, lightly rhythmical

Heart and soul, _____ I fell in love with you. Heart and soul,

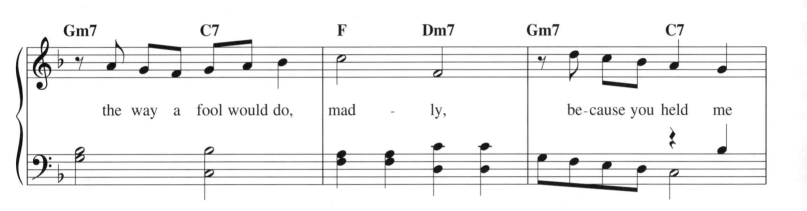

the way a fool would do, mad - ly, be-cause you held me

tight and stole a kiss in the night. Heart and soul, _____

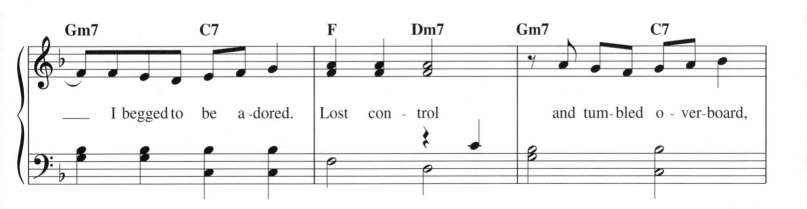

_____ I begged to be a-dored. Lost con - trol and tum-bled o - ver-board,

14

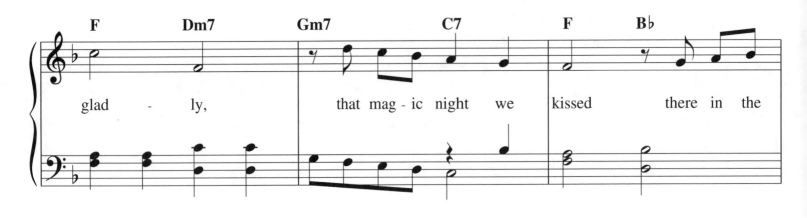

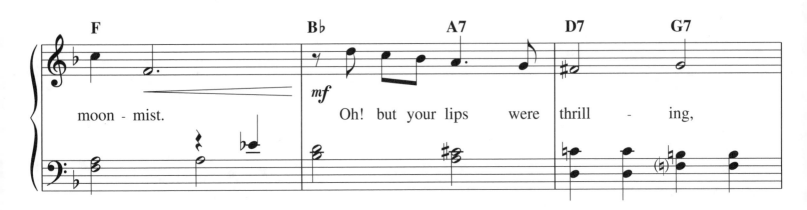

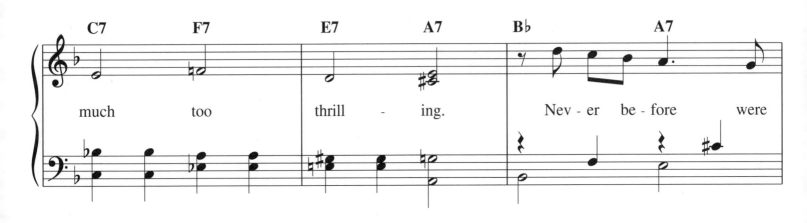

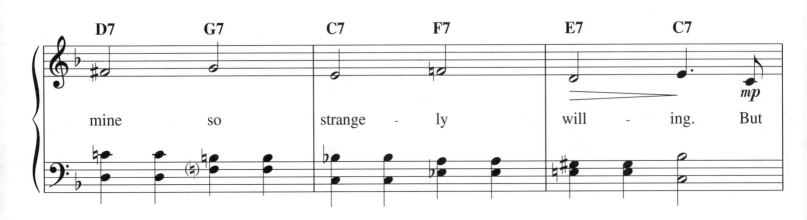

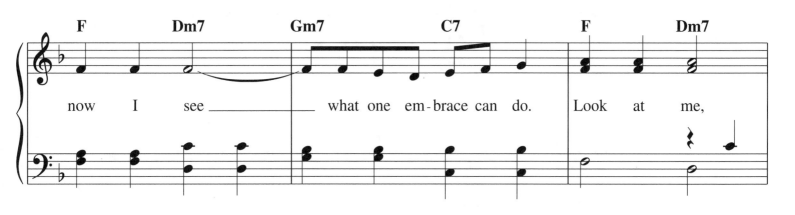

now I see _____ what one em-brace can do. Look at me,

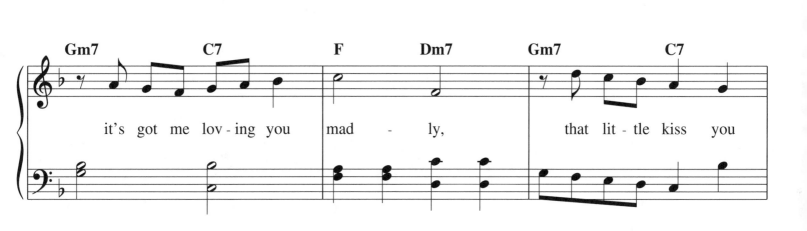

it's got me lov-ing you mad - ly, that lit-tle kiss you

1.

stole held all my heart and soul.

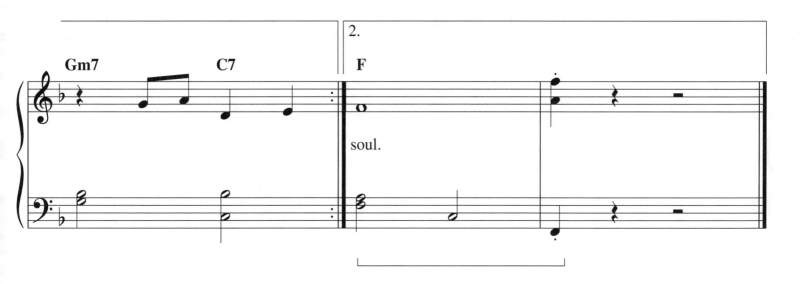

2.

soul.

I GET ALONG WITHOUT YOU VERY WELL
(Except Sometimes)

Words and Music by HOAGY CARMICHAEL
Inspired by a poem written by J.B. THOMPSON

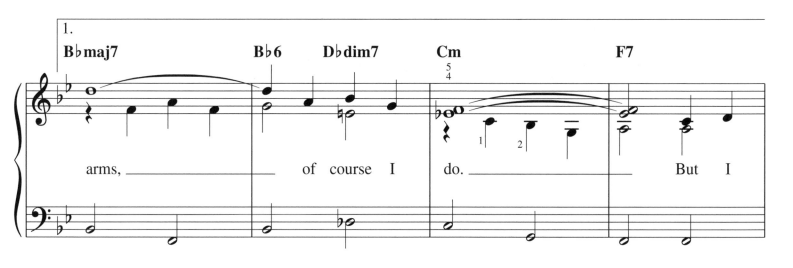

arms, _____ of course I do. _____ But I

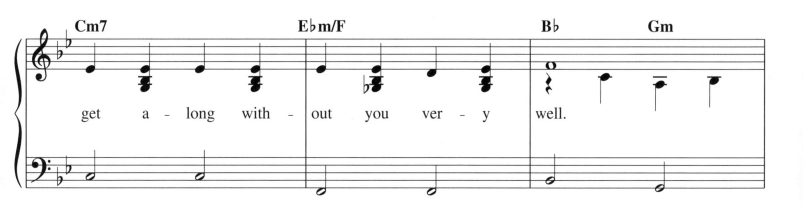

get a - long with - out you ver - y well.

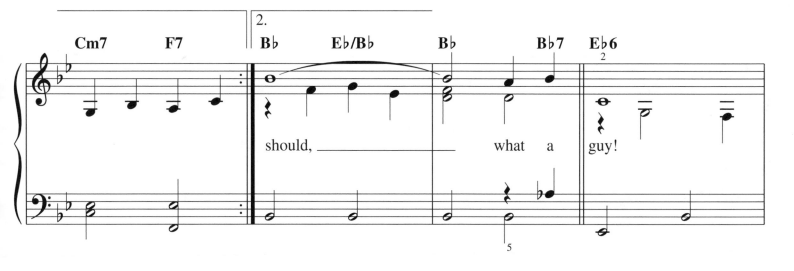

should, _____ what a guy!

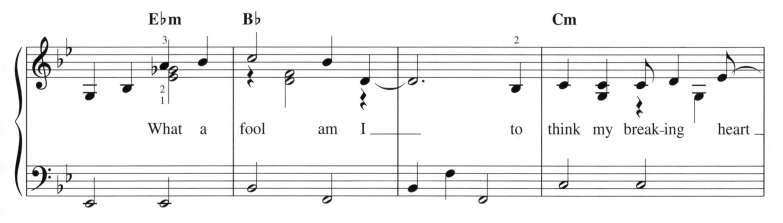

What a fool am I _____ to think my break-ing heart

18

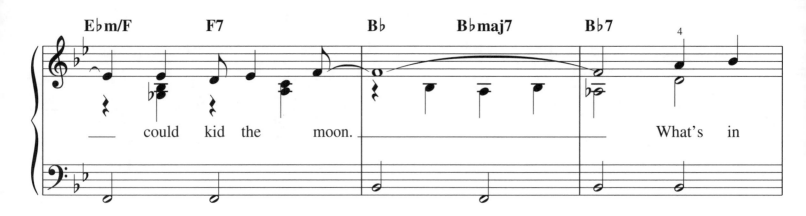

could kid the moon. _____ What's in

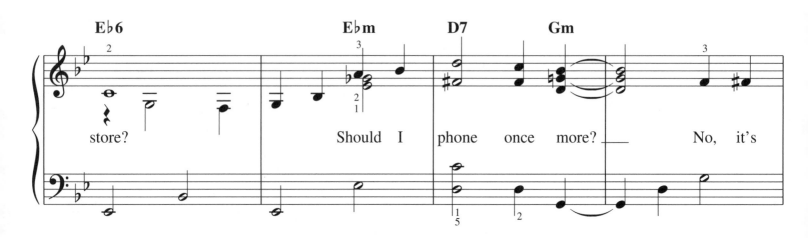

store? Should I phone once more? _____ No, it's

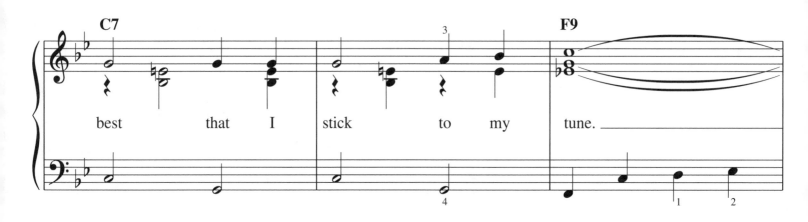

best that I stick to my tune. _____

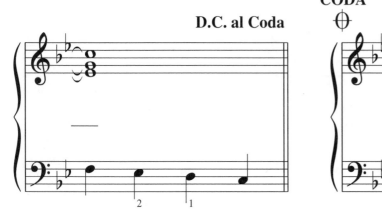

D.C. al Coda

two.

IN THE COOL, COOL, COOL OF THE EVENING

from the Paramount Picture HERE COMES THE GROOM

Words by JOHNNY MERCER
Music by HOAGY CARMICHAEL

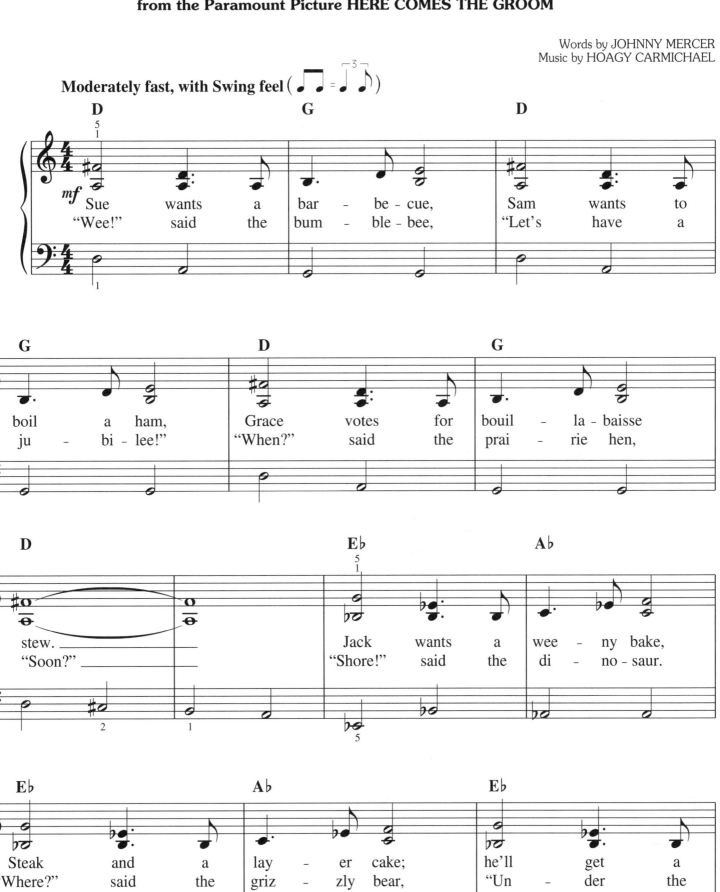

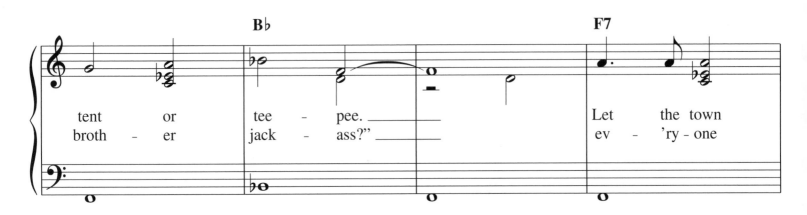

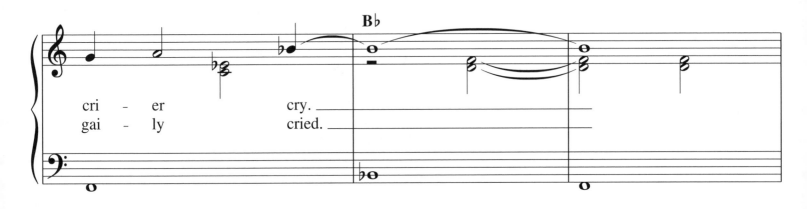

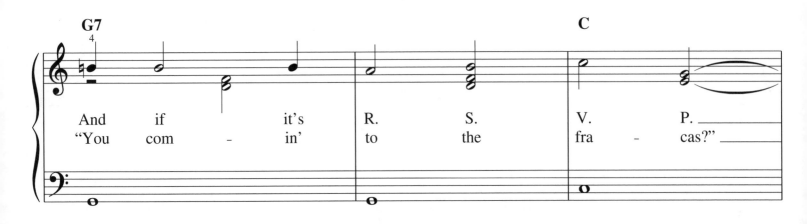

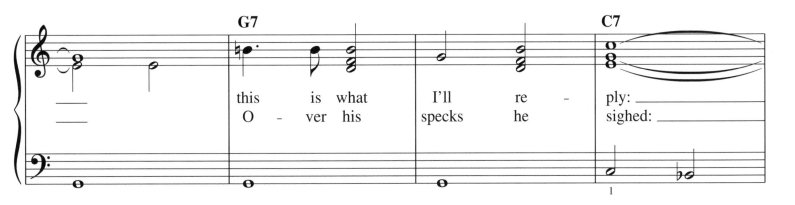

this is what I'll re - ply: ___
O - ver his specks he sighed: ___

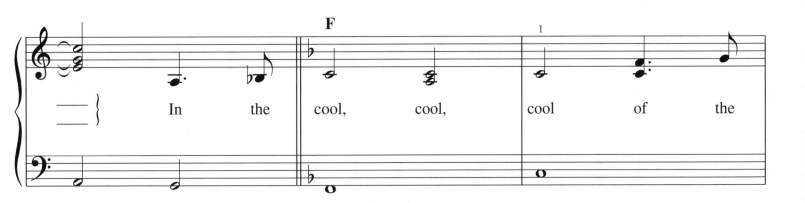

In the cool, cool, cool of the

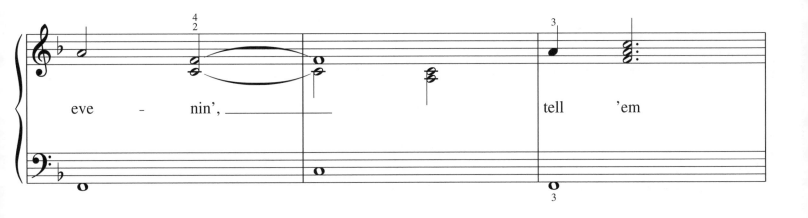

eve - nin', ___ tell 'em

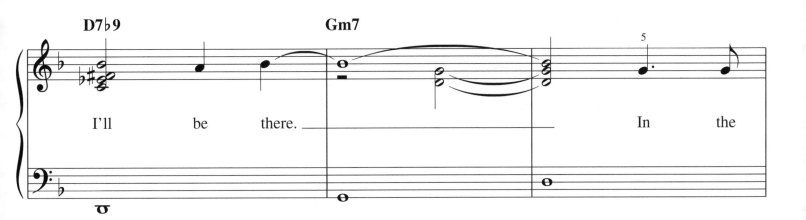

I'll be there. ___ In the

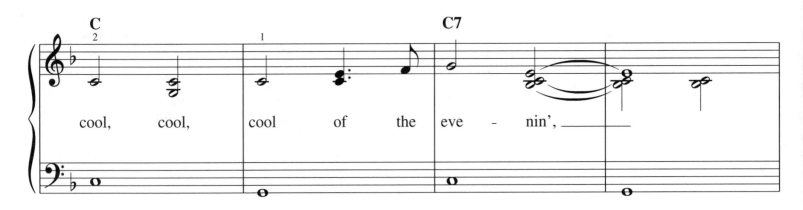

cool,   cool,   cool   of   the   eve - nin', _____

bet - ter   save   a   chair. ____
slick - um   on   my   hair. ____

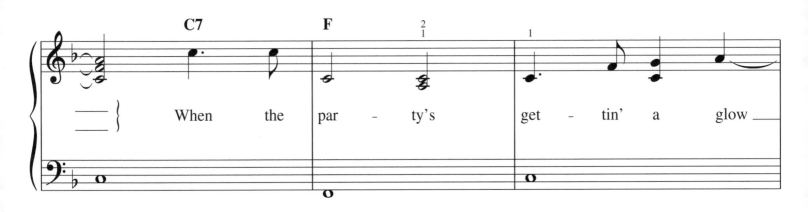

_____   When   the   par - ty's   get - tin'   a   glow ___

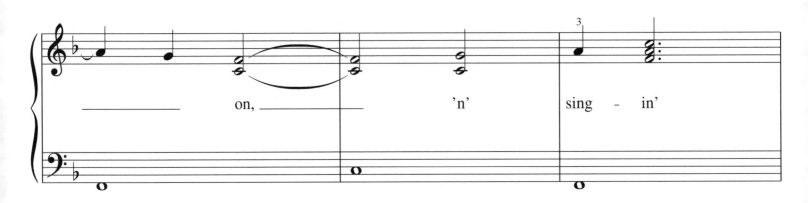

_____   on, _____   'n'   sing - in'

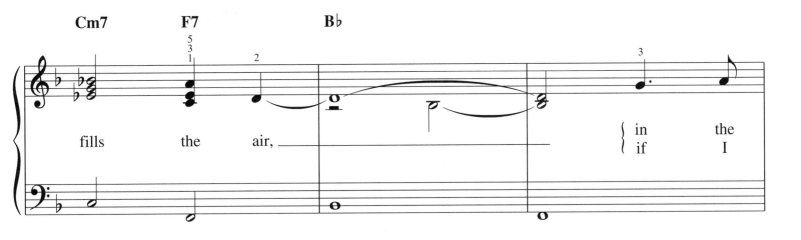

fills the air, _____ in the
                       if I

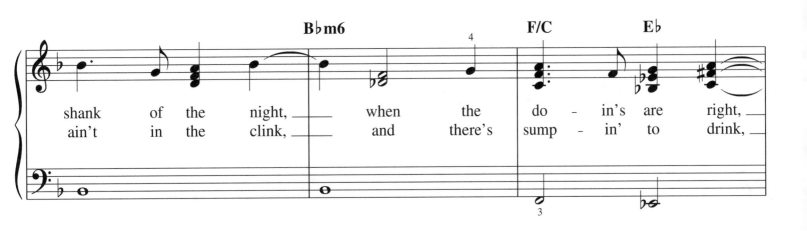

shank of the night, _____ when the do - in's are right, ___
ain't in the clink, _____ and there's sump - in' to drink, ___

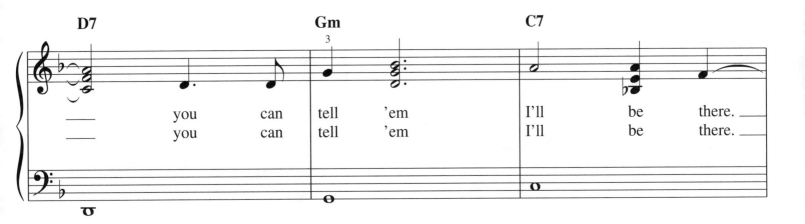

you can tell 'em I'll be there. ____
you can tell 'em I'll be there. ____

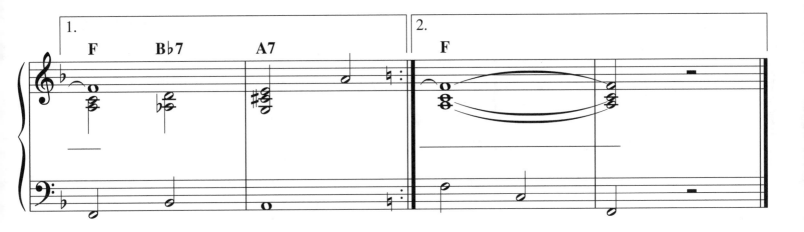

JUNKMAN'S SONG

Words and Music by
HOAGY CARMICHAEL

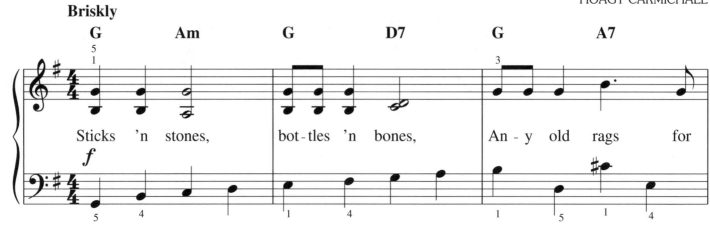

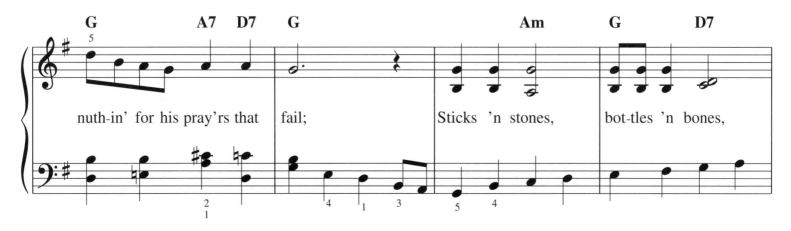

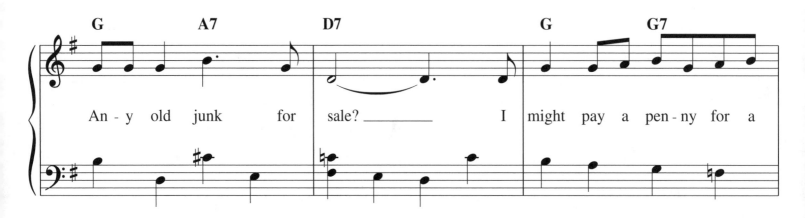

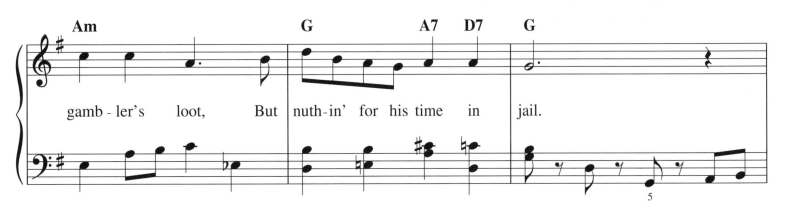

gamb-ler's loot, But nuth-in' for his time in jail.

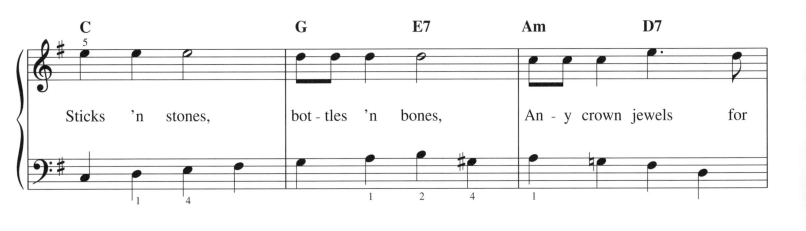

Sticks 'n stones, bot-tles 'n bones, An-y crown jewels for

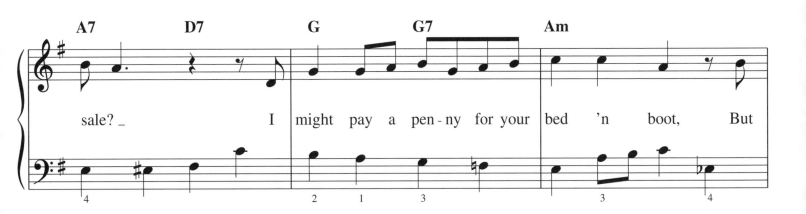

sale? _ I might pay a pen-ny for your bed 'n boot, But

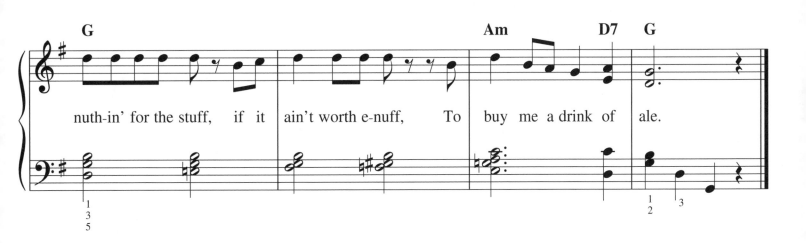

nuth-in' for the stuff, if it ain't worth e-nuff, To buy me a drink of ale.

LAMPLIGHTER'S SERENADE

Words by PAUL FRANCIS WEBSTER
Music by HOAGY CARMICHAEL

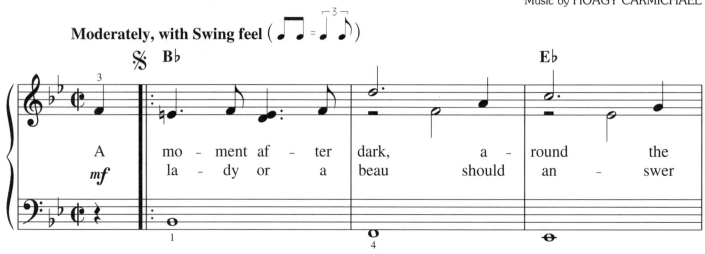

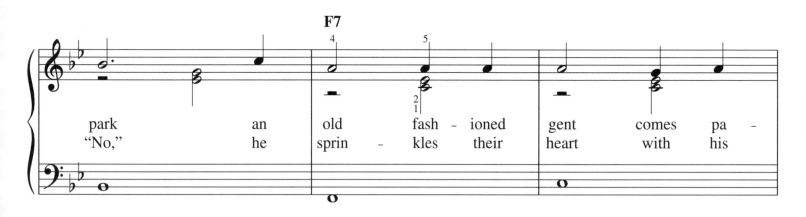

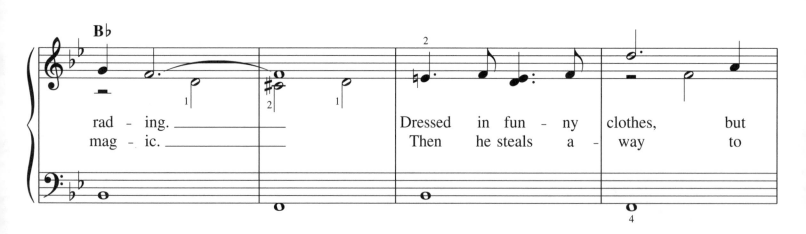

27

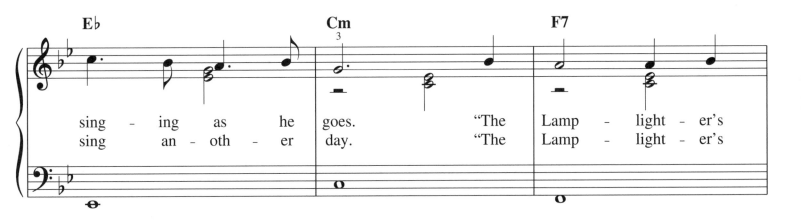

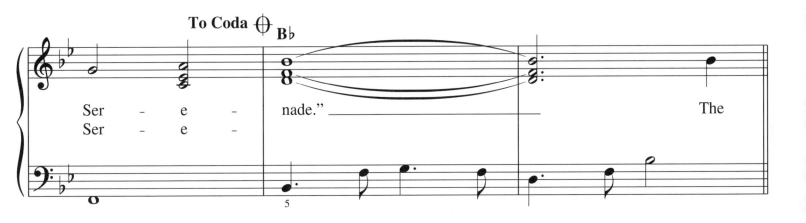

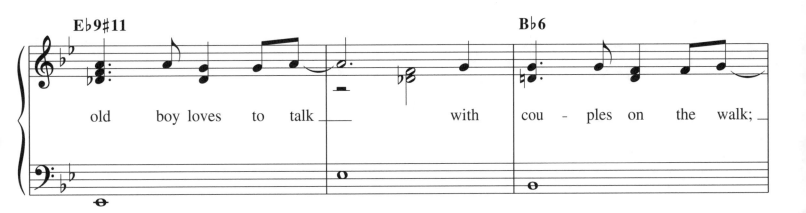

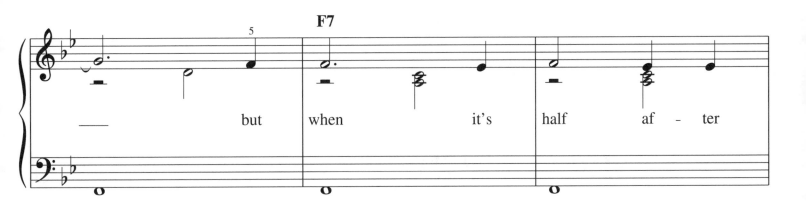

28

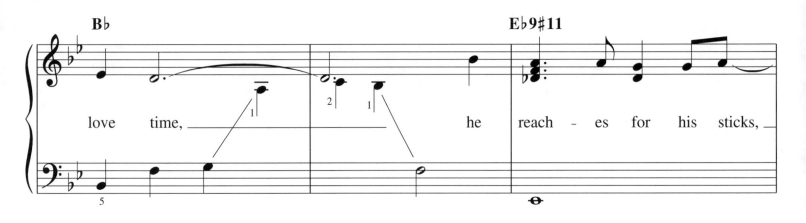

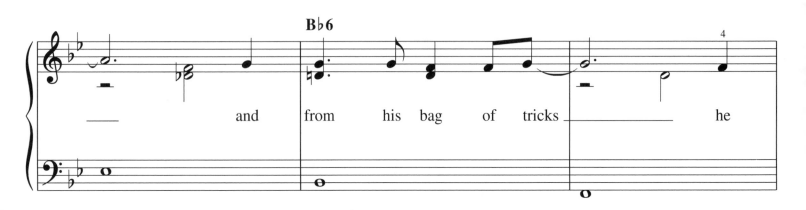

love time, _____ he reach - es for his sticks, _____

and from his bag of tricks _____ he

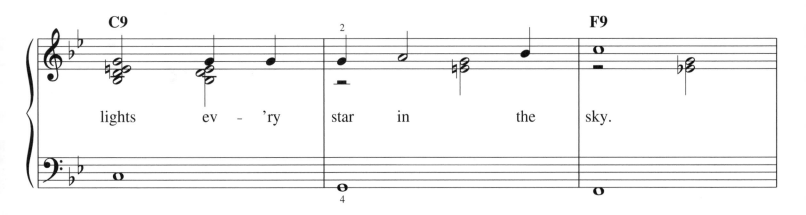

lights ev - 'ry star in the sky.

D.S. al Coda

And if a

CODA

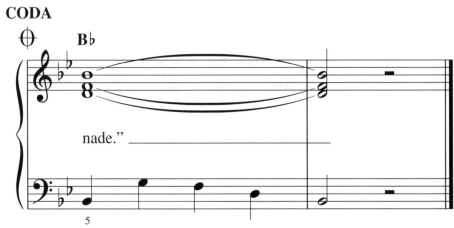

nade." _____

LAZYBONES

Words and Music by HOAGY CARMICHAEL
and JOHNNY MERCER

La - zy-bones,

sleep-in' in the sun, how you 'spec' to get your day's work done?

Nev - er get your day's work done sleep-in' in the noon - day

sun. La - zy-bones, sleep-in' in the shade,

how you 'spec' to get your | corn - meal made? | Nev - er get your corn - meal

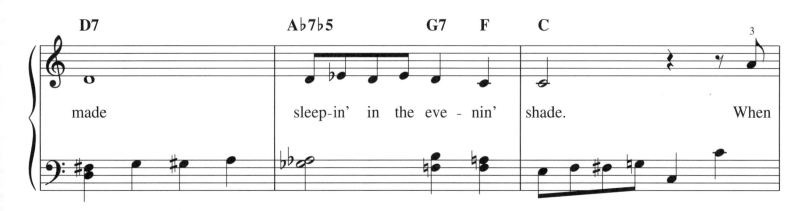

made | sleep-in' in the eve - nin' | shade. When

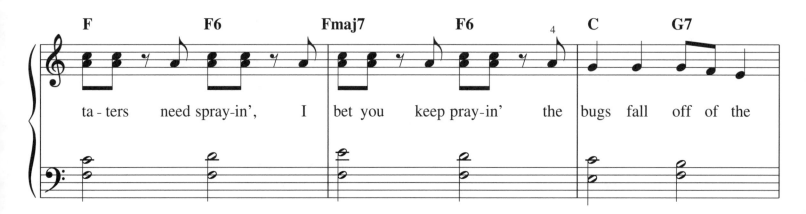

ta - ters need spray-in', I | bet you keep pray-in' the | bugs fall off of the

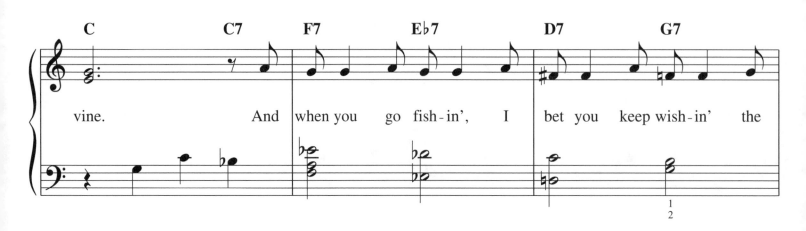

vine. And | when you go fish-in', I | bet you keep wish-in' the

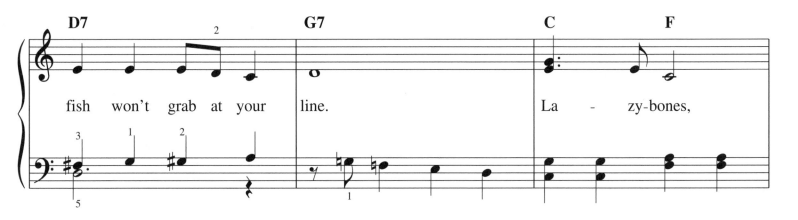

fish won't grab at your line. La - zy-bones,

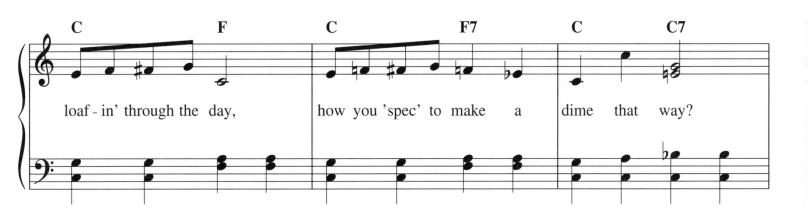

loaf - in' through the day, how you 'spec' to make a dime that way?

Nev - er make a dime that way. Well, look - y here, He nev - er heared a word I

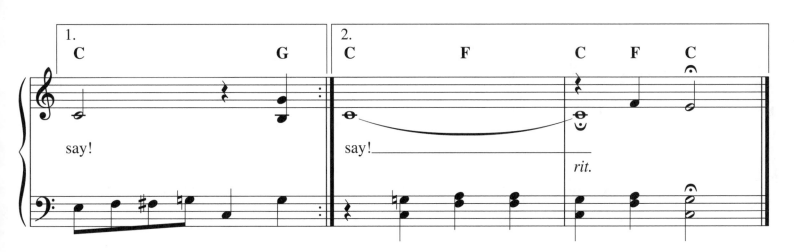

say! say! *rit.*

LAZY RIVER

Words and Music by HOAGY CARMICHAEL
and SIDNEY ARODIN

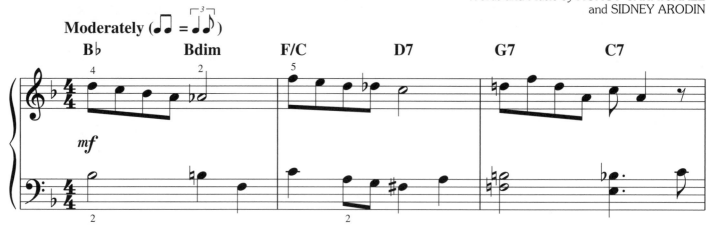

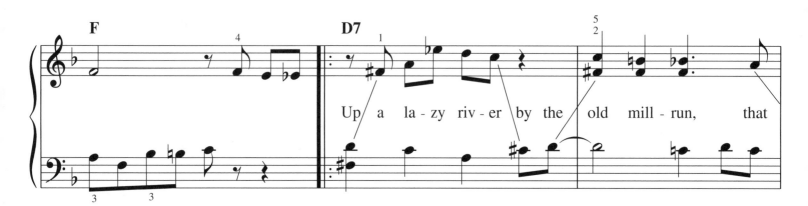

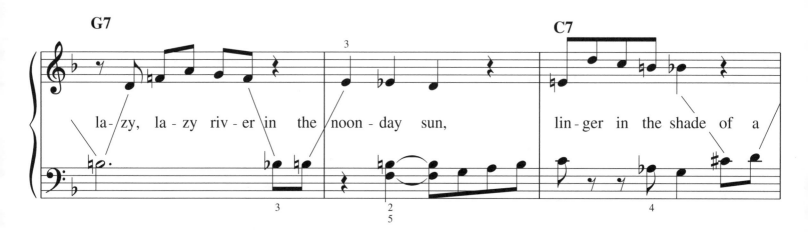

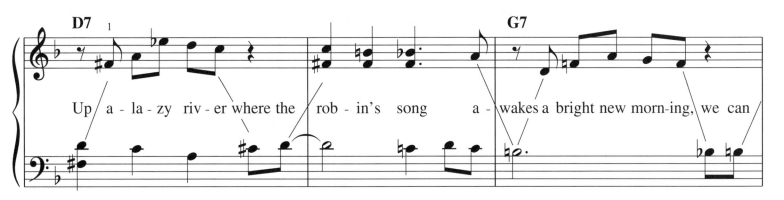

Up / a - la - zy riv - er where the / rob - in's song a - /wakes a bright new morn-ing, we can

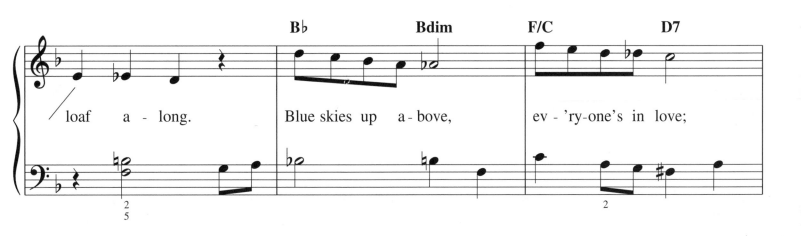

/ loaf a - long. Blue skies up a - bove, ev - 'ry-one's in love;

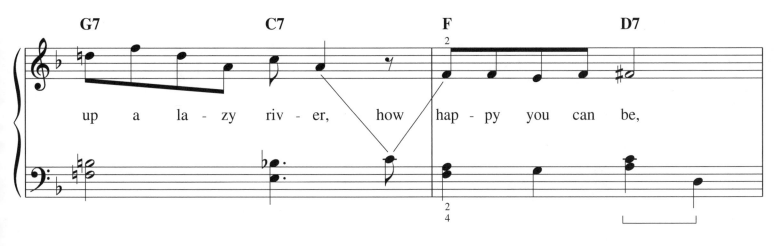

up a la - zy riv - er, how / hap - py you can be,

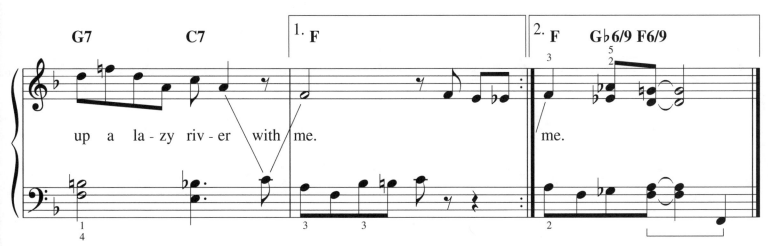

up a la - zy riv - er with / me. me.

34

MERRY GO ROUND

Music by HOAGY CARMICHAEL
Words by MATY MORGAN

Gaily

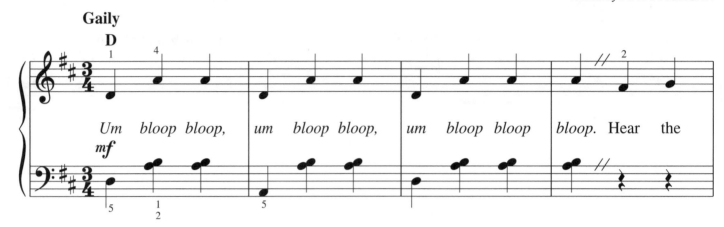

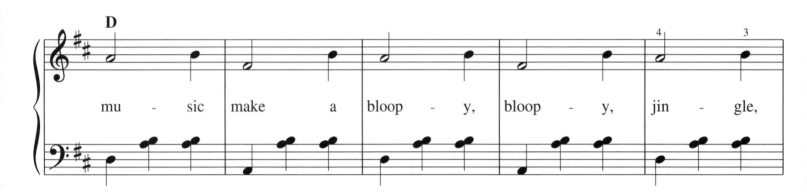

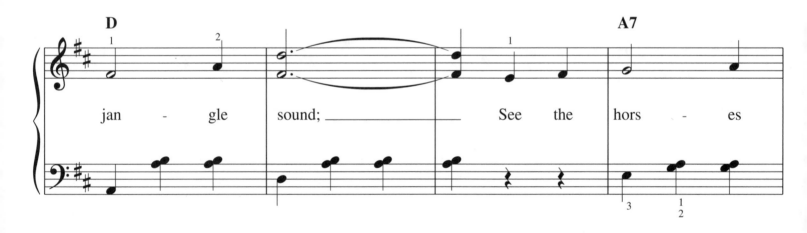

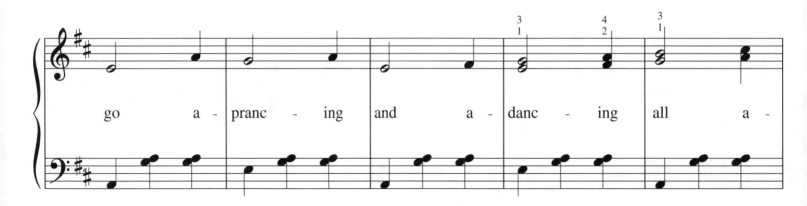

Um bloop bloop, um bloop bloop, um bloop bloop bloop. Hear the music make a bloop-y, bloop-y, jin-gle, jan-gle sound; _____ See the hors-es go a-pranc-ing and a-danc-ing all a-

Copyright © 1957, 1959 and 1971 by Songs Of Peer, Ltd. and Maty Morgan Publishing Designee
Copyrights Renewed
International Copyright Secured All Rights Reserved

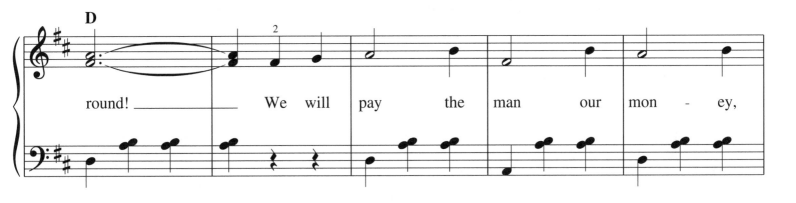

round! _____ We will pay the man our mon - ey,

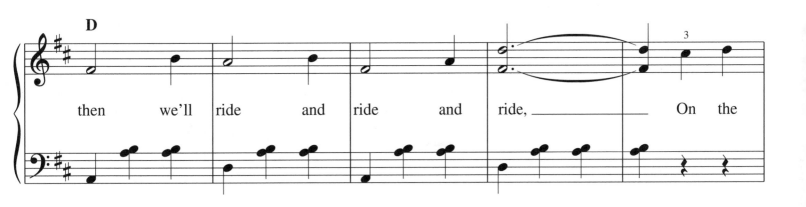

then we'll ride and ride and ride, _____ On the

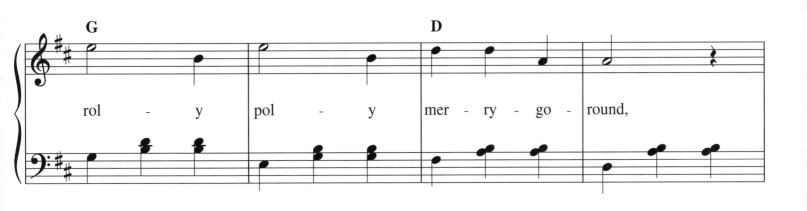

rol - y pol - y mer - ry - go - round,

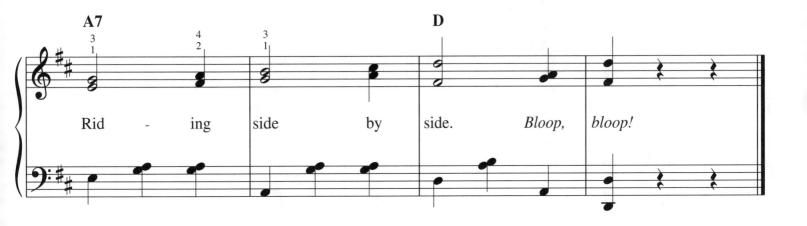

Rid - ing side by side. *Bloop, bloop!*

MY RESISTANCE IS LOW

Words by HAROLD ADAMSON
Music by HOAGY CARMICHAEL

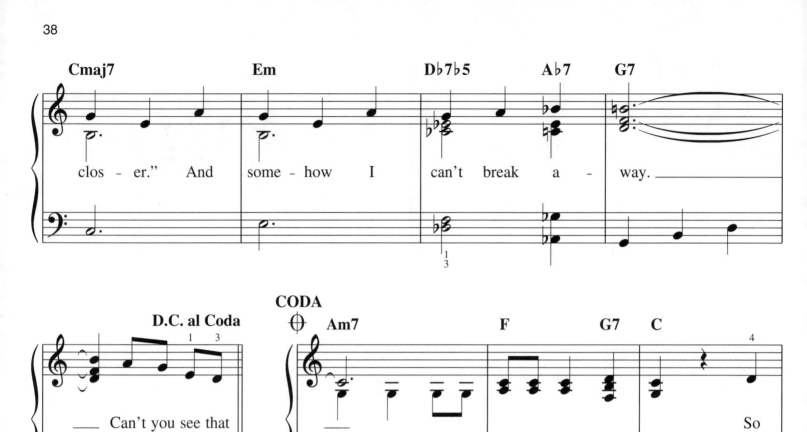

Cmaj7 ... **Em** ... **Db7b5** ... **Ab7** ... **G7**

clos - er." And some - how I can't break a - way. _____

D.C. al Coda

CODA

Am7 ... **F** ... **G7** ... **C**

_____ Can't you see that

So

F ... **Fm** ... **C/E** ... **Am7**

don't be per - sis - tent, please keep your dis - tance, you

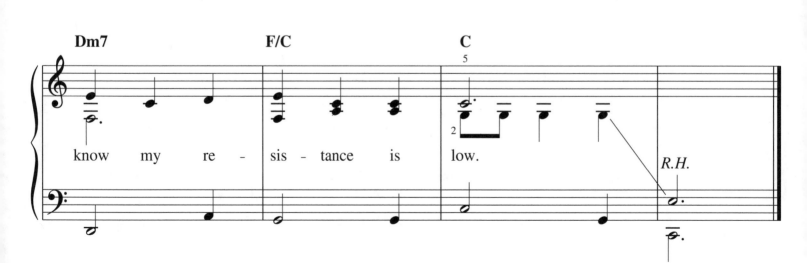

Dm7 ... **F/C** ... **C**

know my re - sis - tance is low.

R.H.

THE OLD PROSPECTOR

Words and Music by
HOAGY CARMICHAEL

Wistfully

Me an' my lit - tle don - key ___ are go - in' some place, ___
We know it's cold - er'n blaz - es ___ a - head up a piece, ___

We don't know where or how far;
Some - how, we nei - ther one care,

We've set our sights on the north - ern lights,
If we "go broke," you can "bet your poke,"

1. Hop - in' we'll find a star.
   Heav - en is wait - in'

2. there.

OLE BUTTERMILK SKY

from the Motion Picture CANYON PASSAGE

Words and Music by HOAGY CARMICHAEL
and JACK BROOKS

42

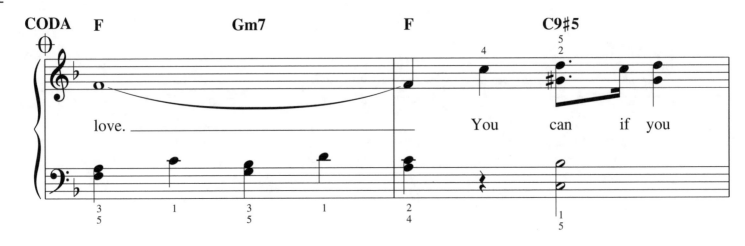

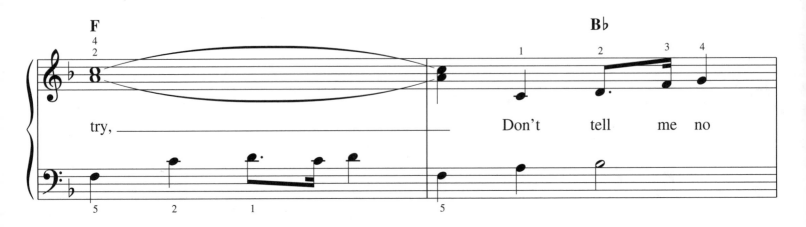

ROCKET SHIP

Words and Music by
HOAGY CARMICHAEL

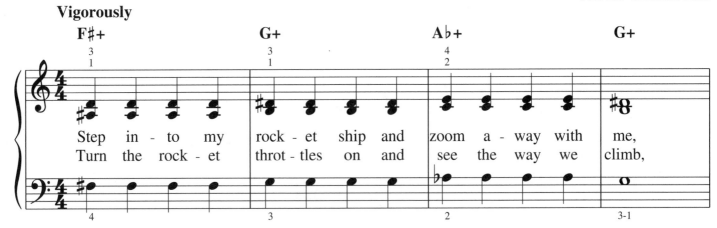

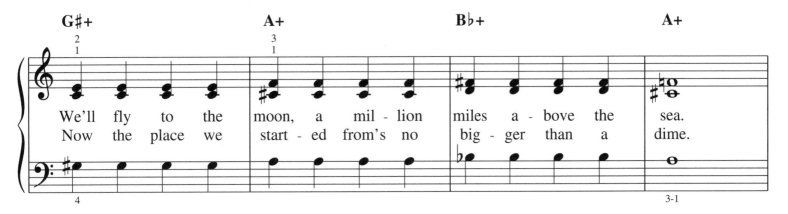

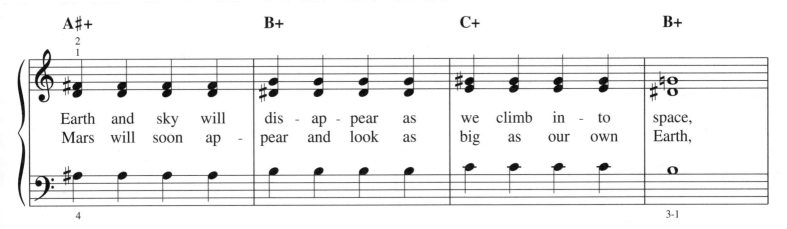

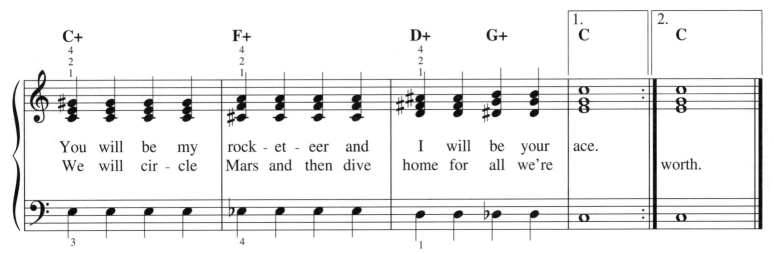

RAFFLES

Words and Music by
HOAGY CARMICHAEL

Smoothly

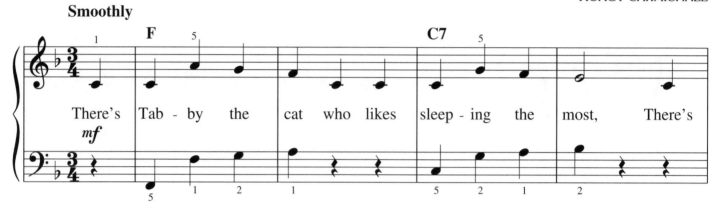

There's Tab-by the cat who likes sleep-ing the most, There's

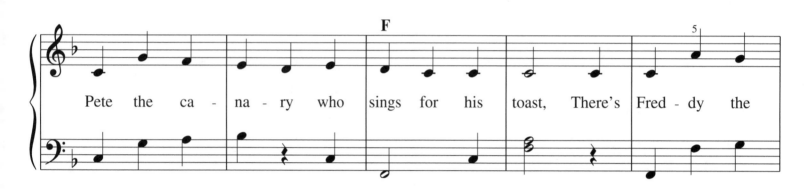

Pete the ca-na-ry who sings for his toast, There's Fred-dy the

frog who jumps o-ver my hat, Rab-bits and gold-fish and

pets such as that; And then there is one that I've not men-tioned

45

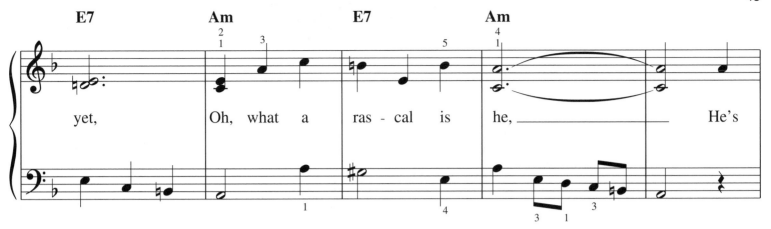

yet, Oh, what a ras - cal is he, _____ He's

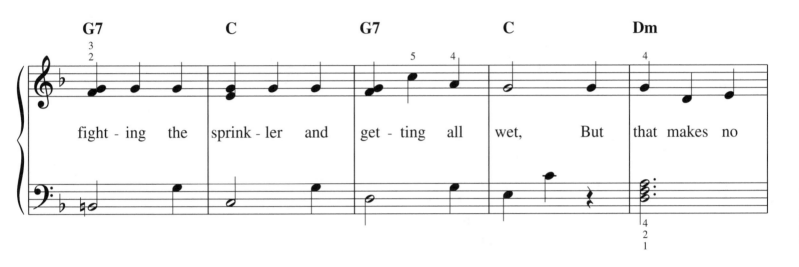

fight - ing the sprink - ler and get - ting all wet, But that makes no

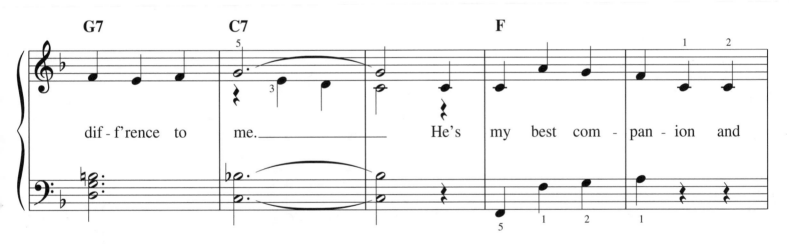

dif - f'rence to me. _____ He's my best com - pan - ion and

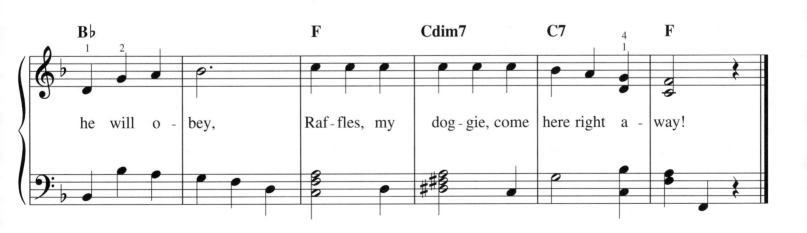

he will o - bey, Raf - fles, my dog - gie, come here right a - way!

ROCKIN' CHAIR

Words and Music by
HOAGY CARMICHAEL

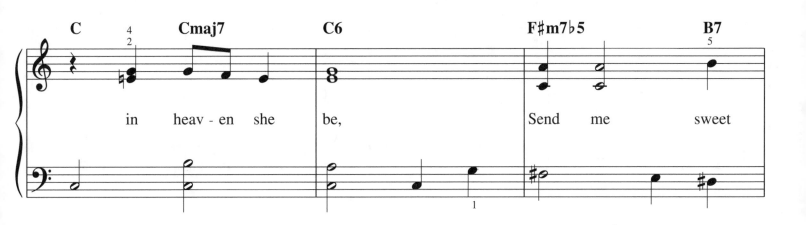

48

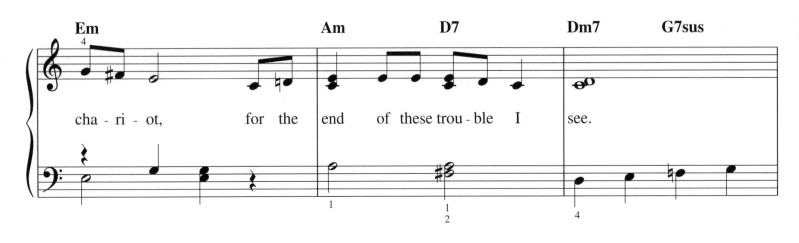

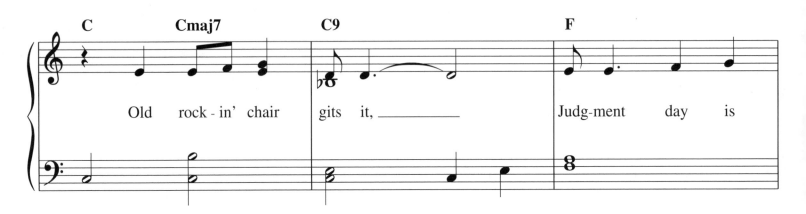

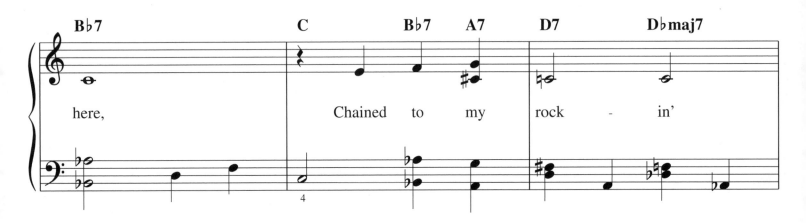

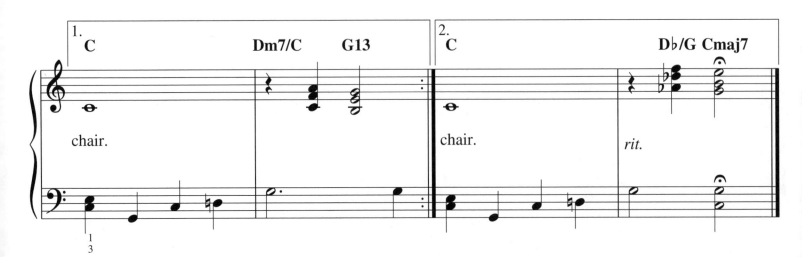

SMALL FRY

from the Paramount Picture SING, YOU SINNERS

Words by FRANK LOESSER
Music by HOAGY CARMICHAEL

ain't a grown-up, high and might-y yet. Small fry,
Small fry, you

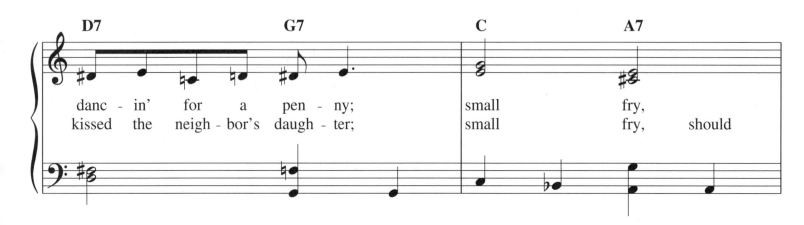

danc - in' for a pen - ny; small fry,
kissed the neigh - bor's daugh - ter; small fry, should

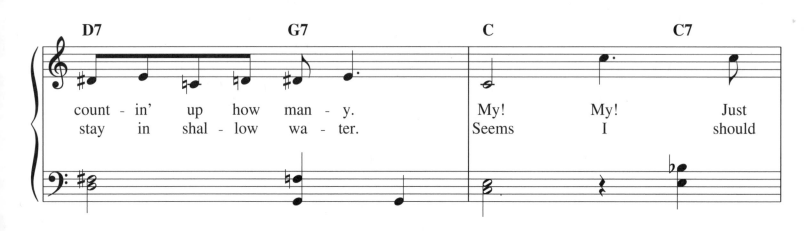

count - in' up how man - y. My! My! Just
stay in shal - low wa - ter. Seems I should

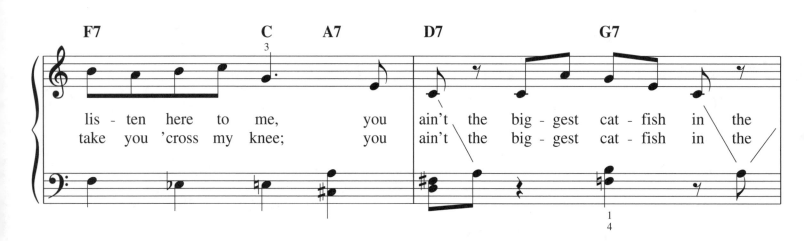

lis - ten here to me, you ain't the big - gest cat - fish in the
take you 'cross my knee; you ain't the big - gest cat - fish in the

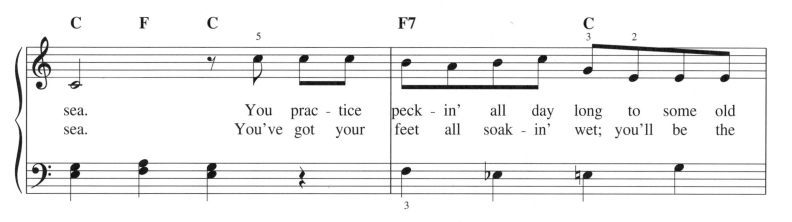

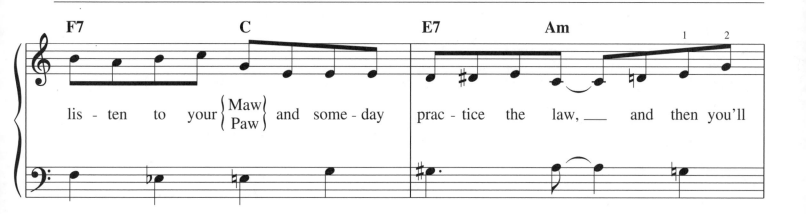

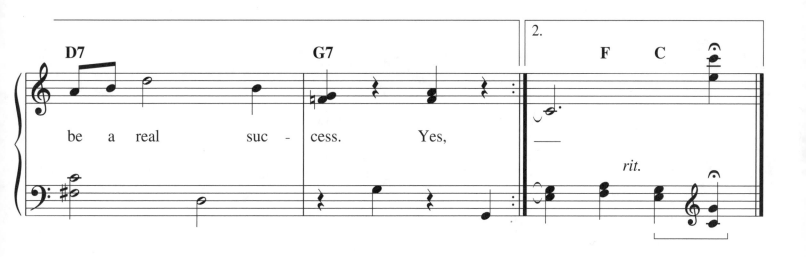

STAR DUST

Words by MITCHELL PARISH
Music by HOAGY CARMICHAEL

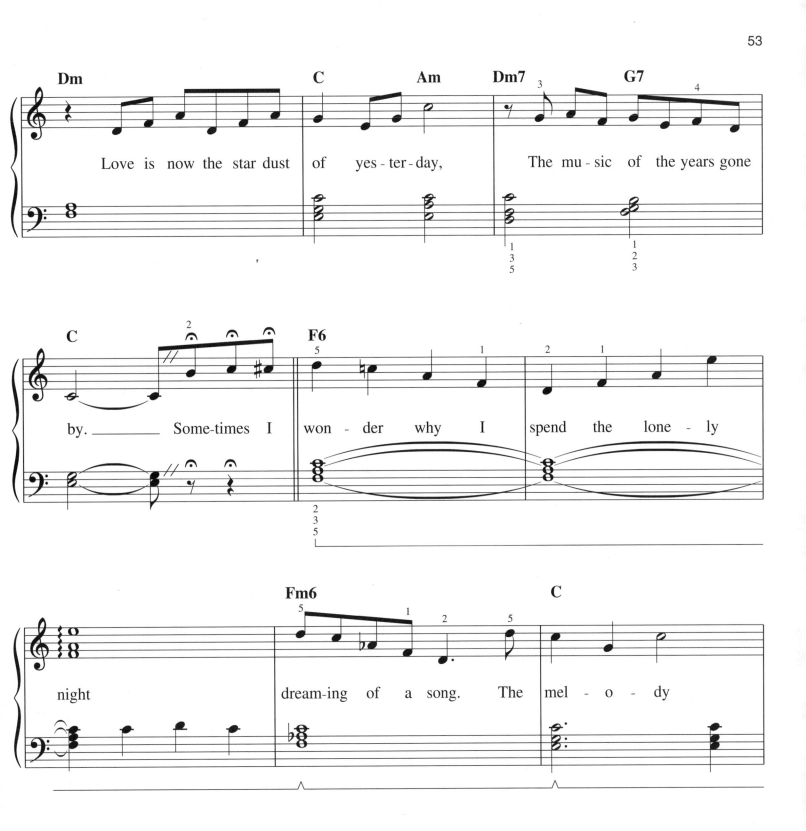

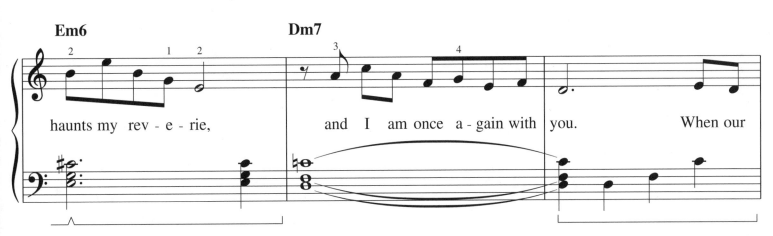

love was new and each kiss an in - spi - ra - tion,

But that was ong a - go, Now my con - sol - a - tion is

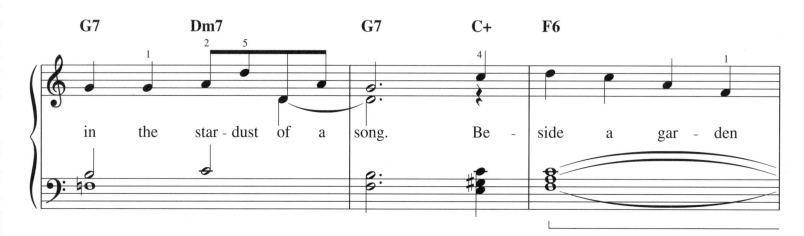

in the star - dust of a song. Be - side a gar - den

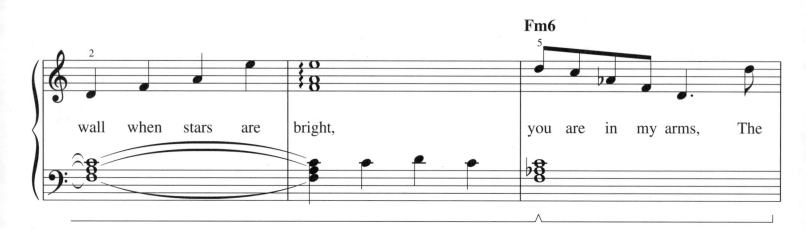

wall when stars are bright, you are in my arms, The

night - in - gale   tells his fair - y tale   of par - a - dise where ros - es

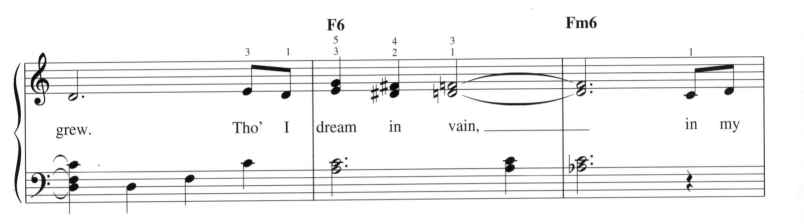

grew.   Tho' I   dream   in   vain, _____   in my

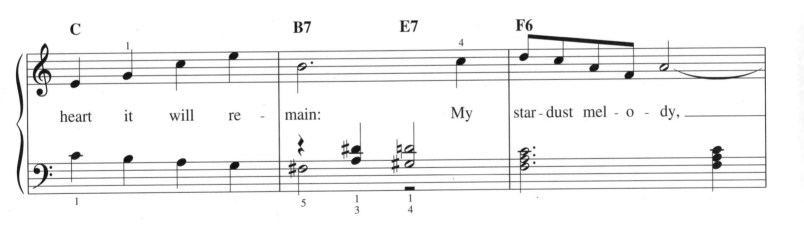

heart   it   will   re - main: My   star - dust mel - o - dy, _____

_____ the mem - o - ry   of love's re - frain.
rall.

SWING HIGH

Words and Music by HOAGY CARMICHAEL
and PATIENCE STRONG

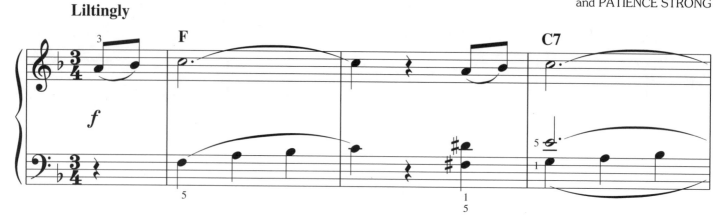

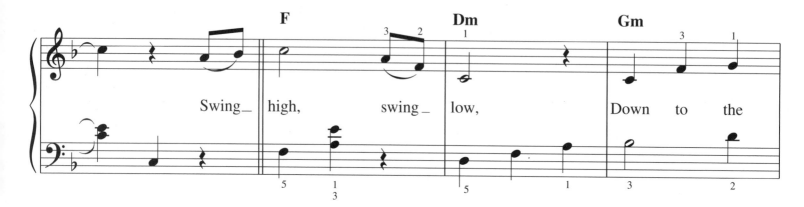

Swing__ high, swing__ low, Down to the

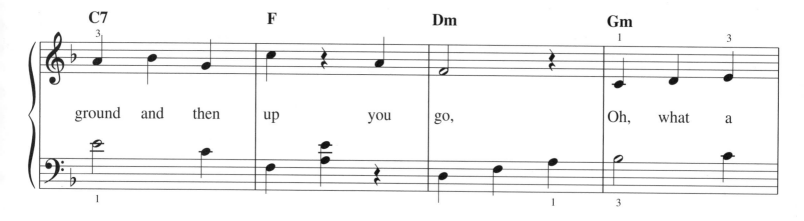

ground and then up you go, Oh, what a

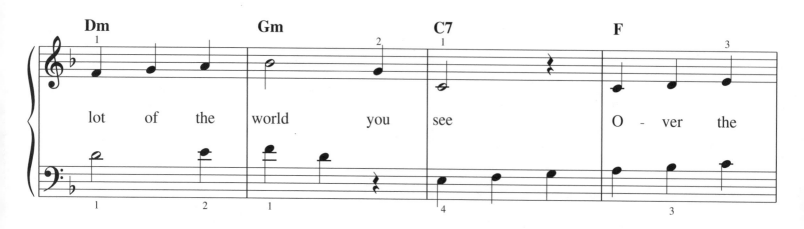

lot of the world you see Over the

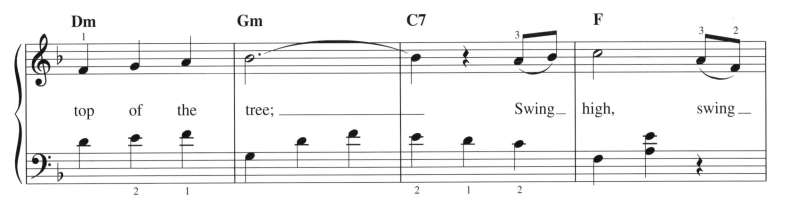

top of the tree; _____ Swing_ high, swing _

low, just like a bird on the wing you

go, But what if the swing __ should swing __ you

high, And leave you up there in the sky? _____

THIRTY DAYS HATH SEPTEMBER

Words and Music by
HOAGY CARMICHAEL

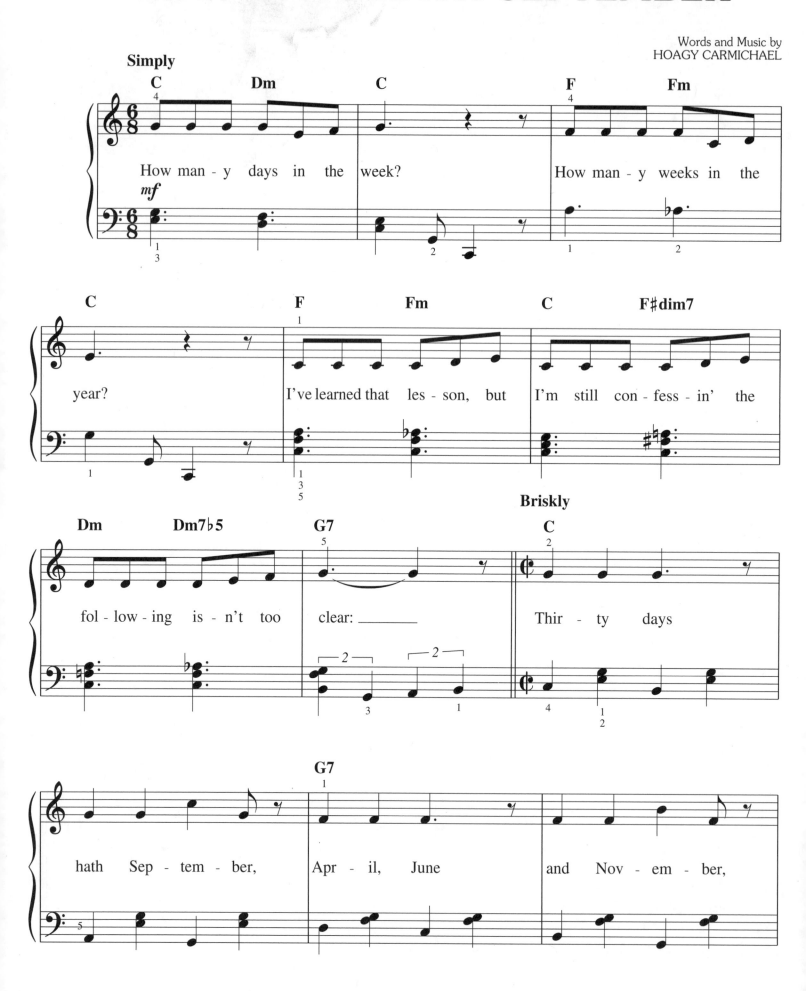

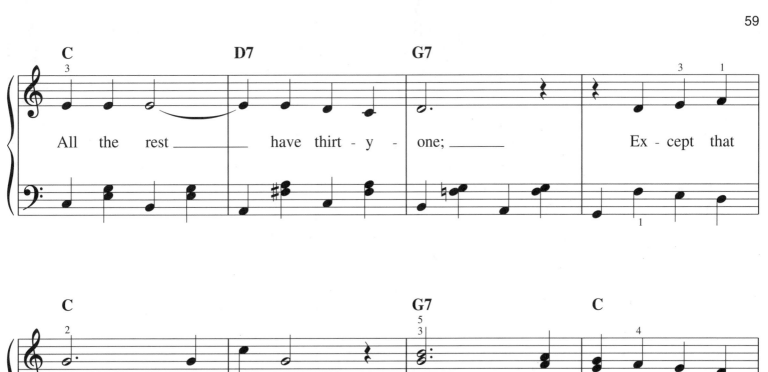

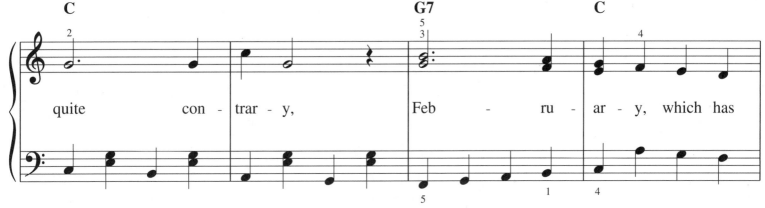

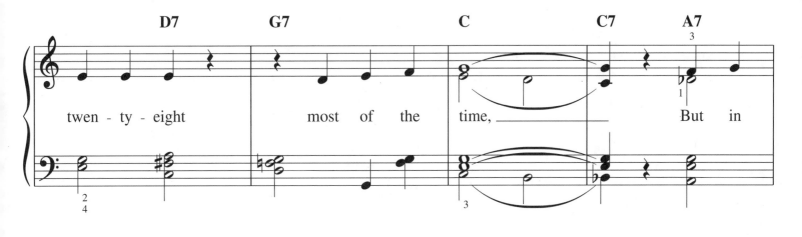

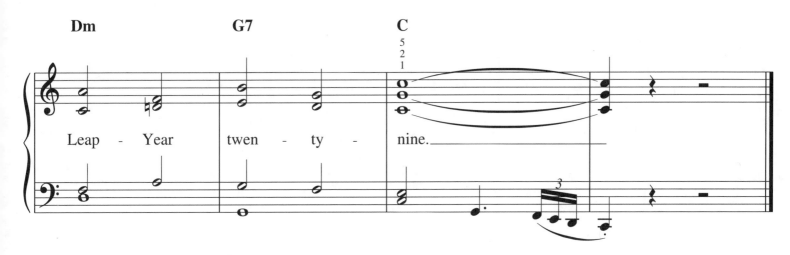

TRAVELING

Words and Music by
HOAGY CARMICHAEL

Brightly

Trav - 'ling is fun for a
Sail - boats are jol - ly when

hol - i - day kick, You'll like the
there's a stiff breeze, If you're not

curves and the get - tin' there
search - ing for birds' nests and

quick, Air - planes and aut - os can
bees, I still like walk - ing when

beat   an - y   bike,   But   can   they

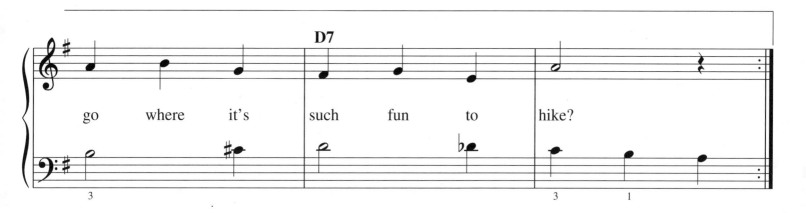

go   where   it's   such   fun   to   hike?

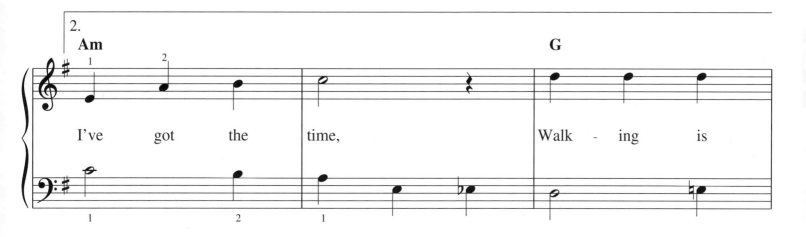

I've   got   the   time,   Walk - ing   is

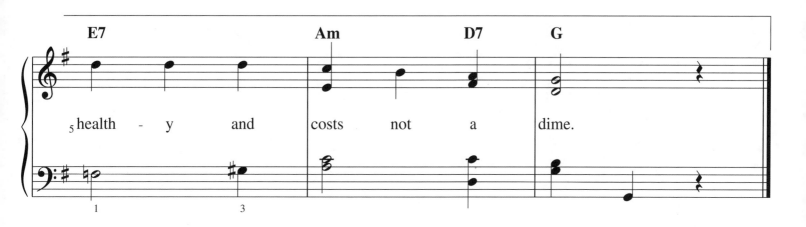

health - y   and   costs   not   a   dime.

THE WHALE SONG

Words and Music by HOAGY CARMICHAEL
and GEOFFREY DEARMER

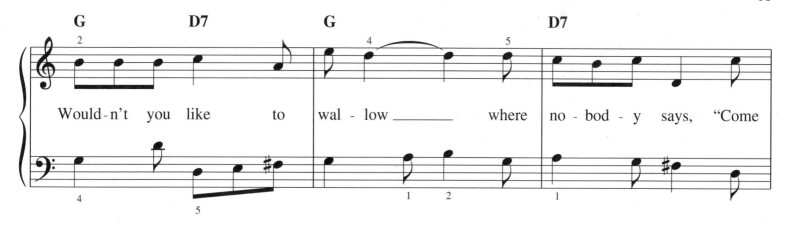

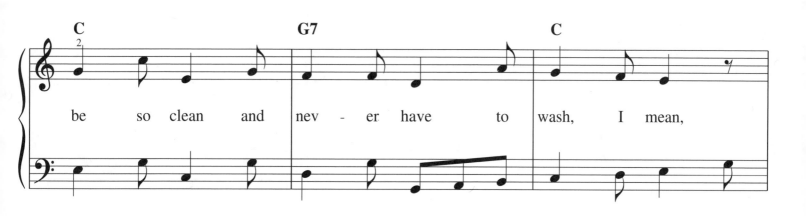

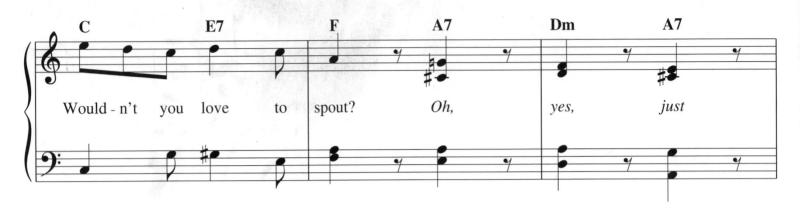

Would - n't you love to spout? *Oh,* *yes,* *just*

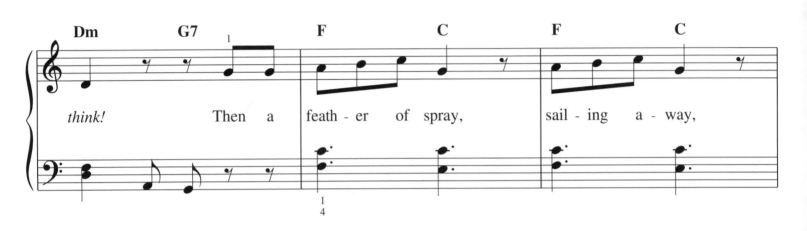

think! Then a feath - er of spray, sail - ing a - way,

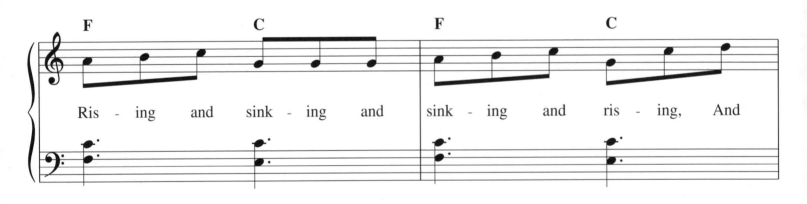

Ris - ing and sink - ing and sink - ing and ris - ing, And

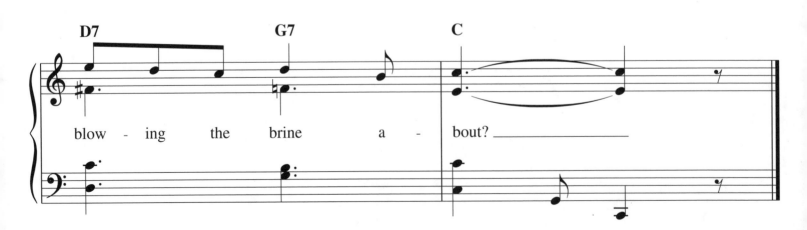

blow - ing the brine a - bout? _____